THERE'S SNOW ON

THE MOUNTAIN

AS PHOTOGRAPHED BY

LARRY STIMELING

THERE'S SNOW ON THE MOUNTAIN

AS PHOTOGRAPHED BY

LARRY STIMELING

With Eternal Love

And Deep Gratitude

To

Johne Shelabarger

Without whom this book would not

have been possible

I moves to Arizona in November of 2013. The reason I left the Midwest was, of course, female. I was given a chance to be with the woman I fell in love with over forty years earlier.

An added benefit was I was able to get away from the harsh Midwestern weather.

I carried mail in those long cold winters for thirty-three years. That seemed to be thirty-four years too long!

Then it happened. On New Year's Day 2015 the love of my life said to me, "There's snow on the mountain." Here I thought I had seen my last of that four-letter-word. But no it was true. There was snow on the mountain.

The good thing about snow on the mountain is ... Well there are many good things. One is you do not have to shovel it. Another is you can view it from long distance. And three it makes for some very beautiful pictures.

We went out and took some of those shots.

I am still glad I moved away from the Midwest and its snow but I am also glad for the days when I can look to the east and see that "There's snow on the mountain".

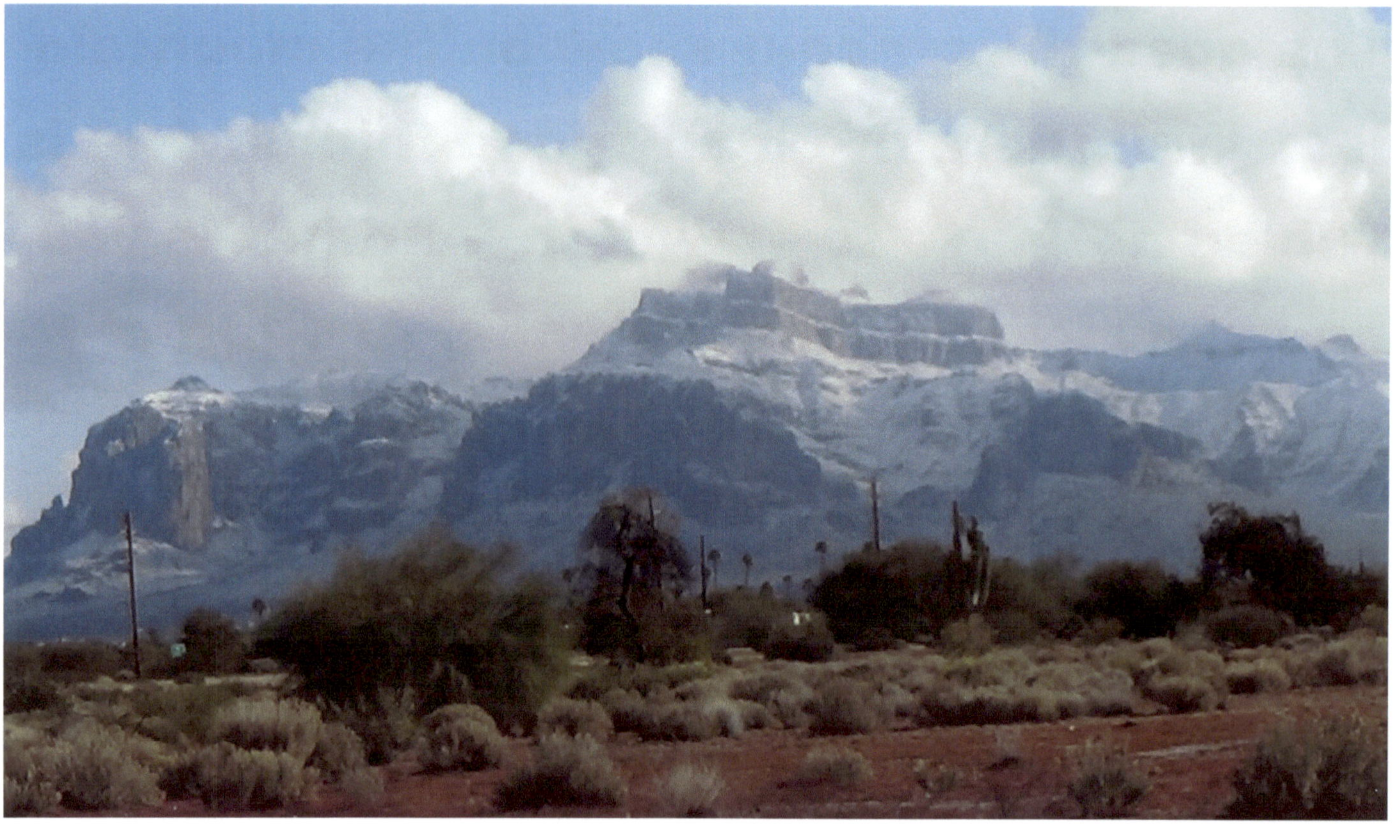

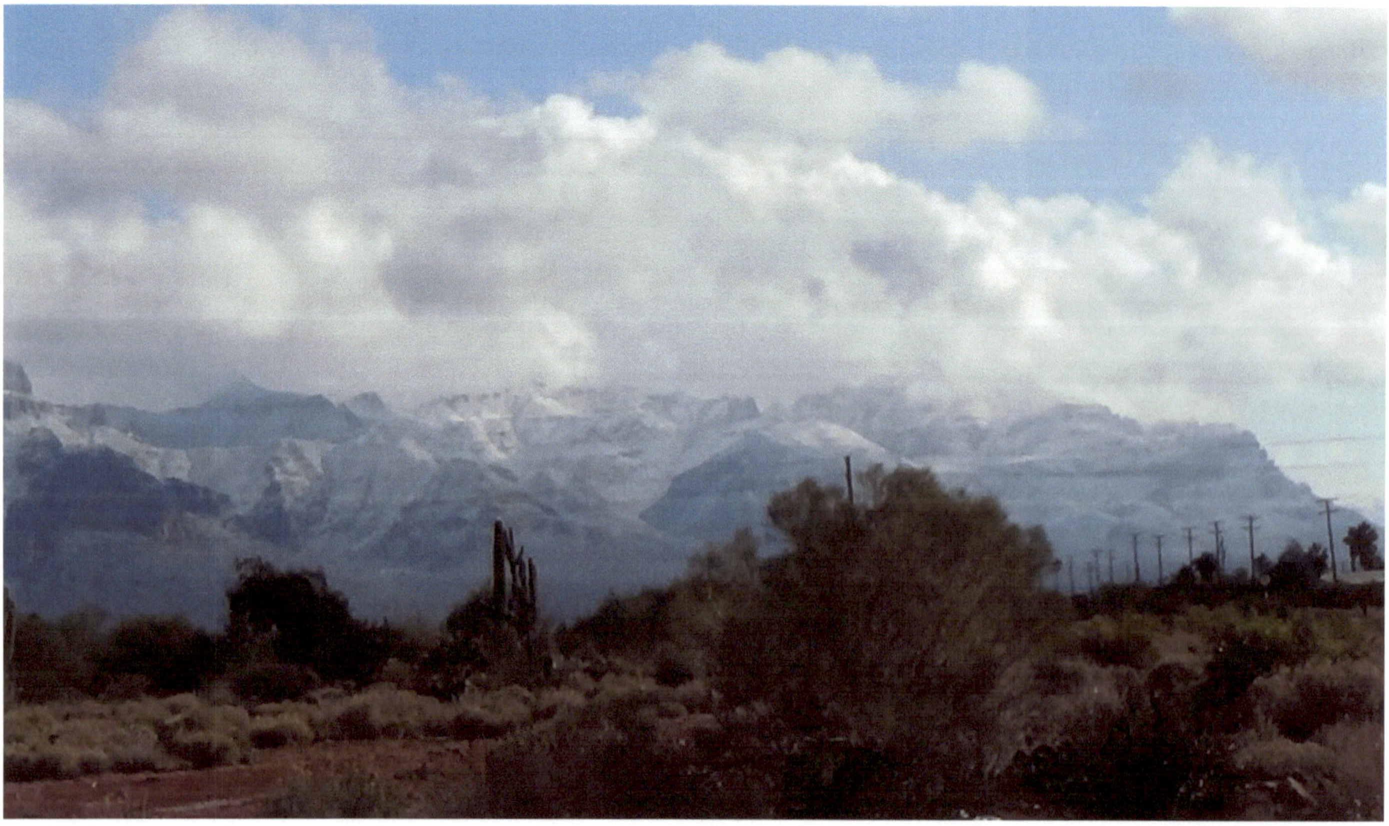

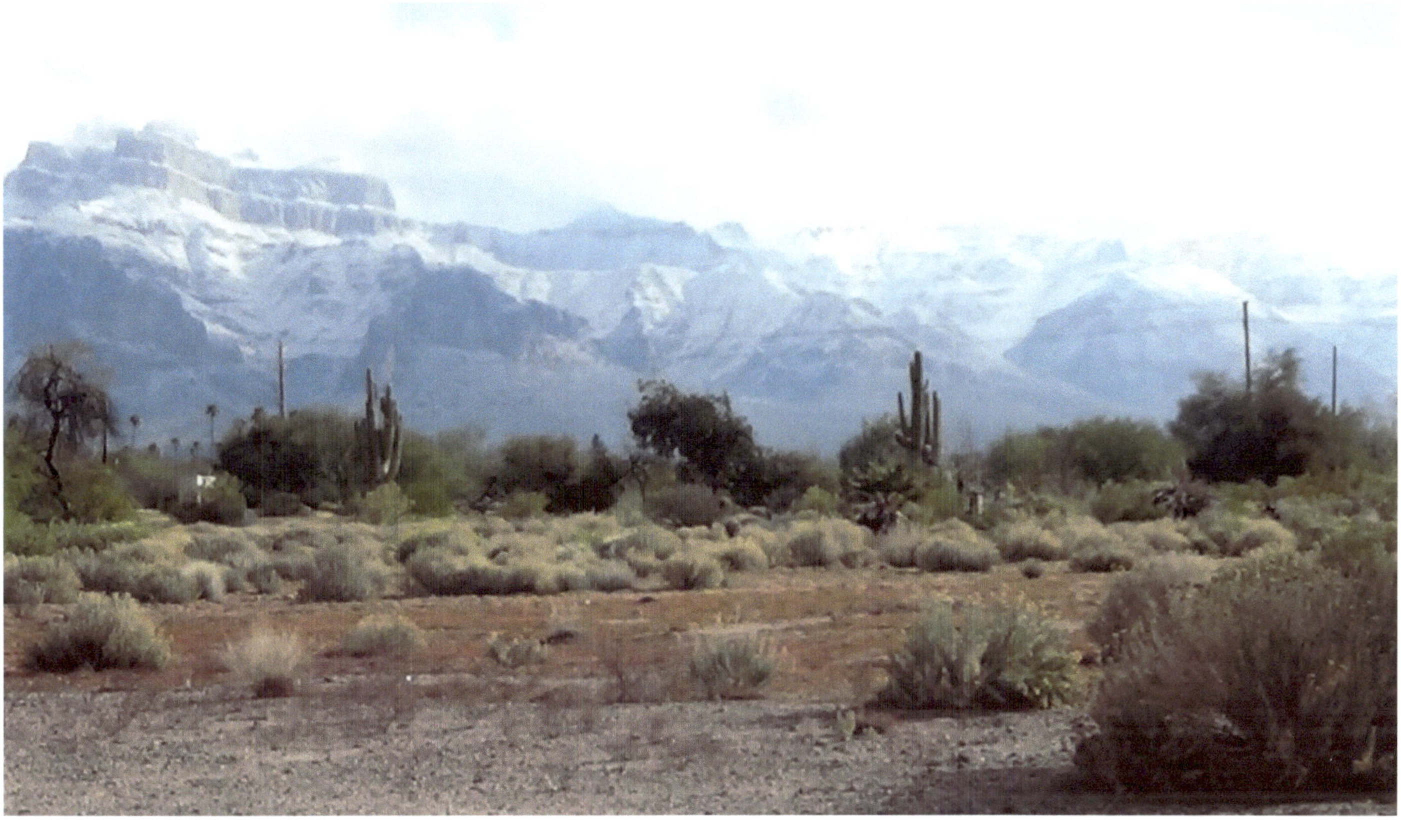

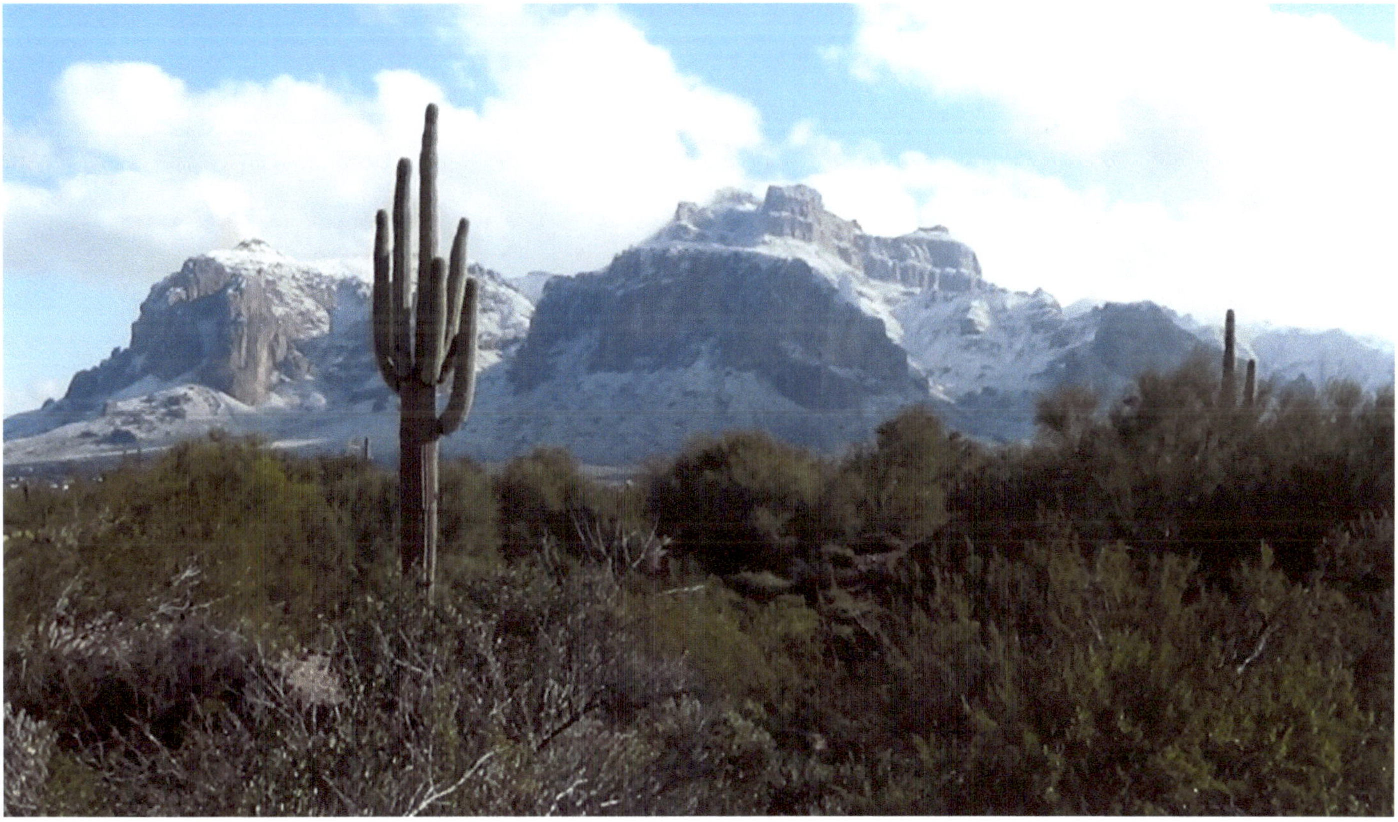

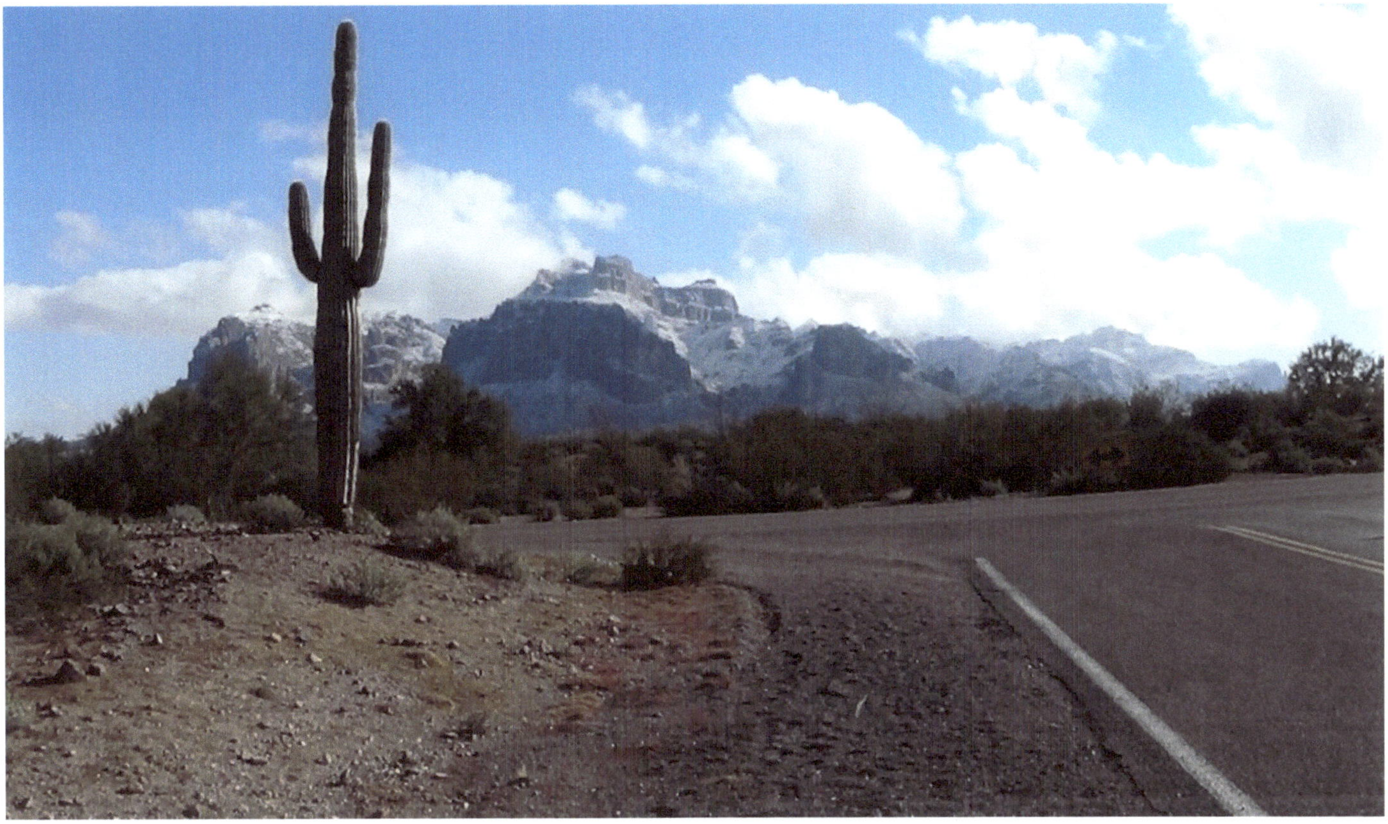

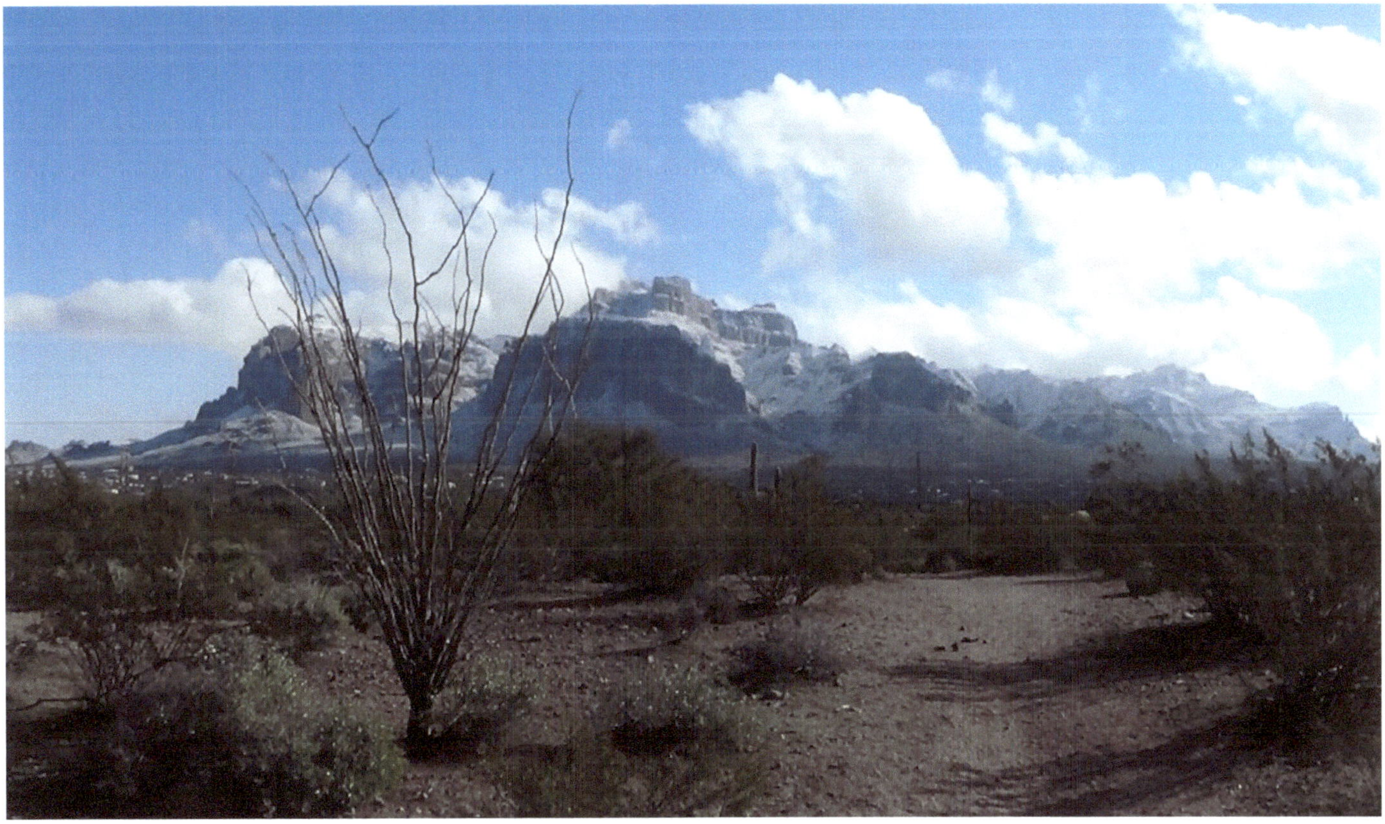

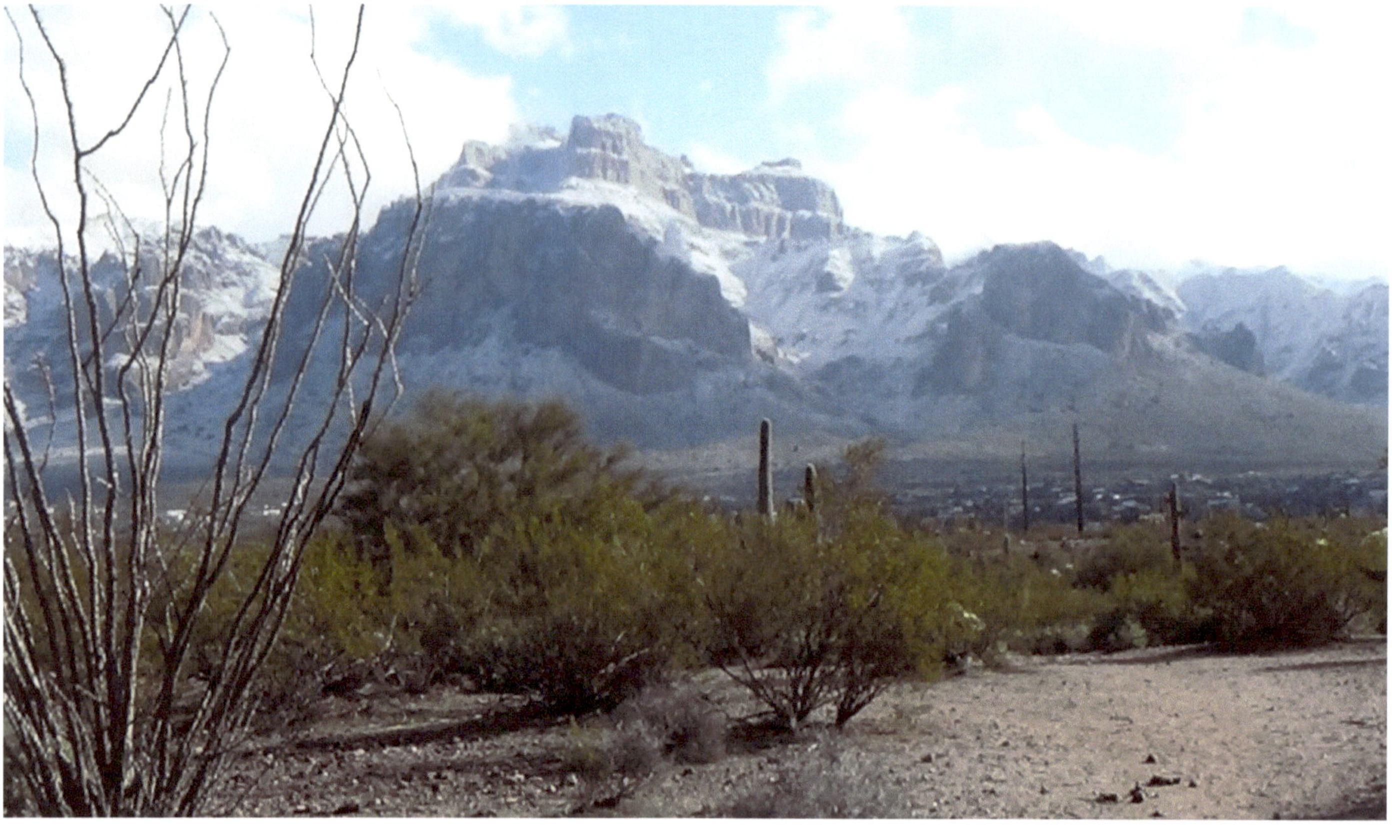

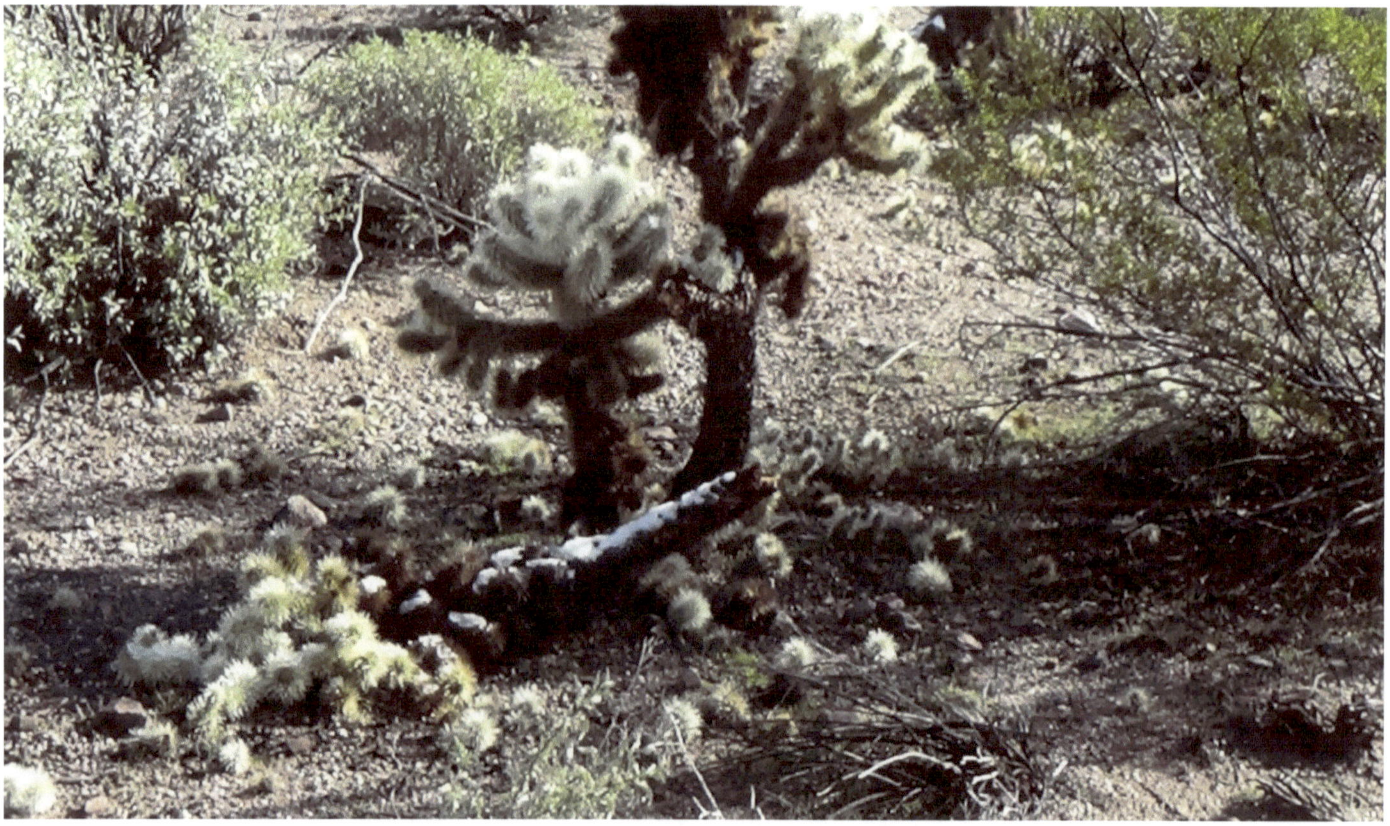

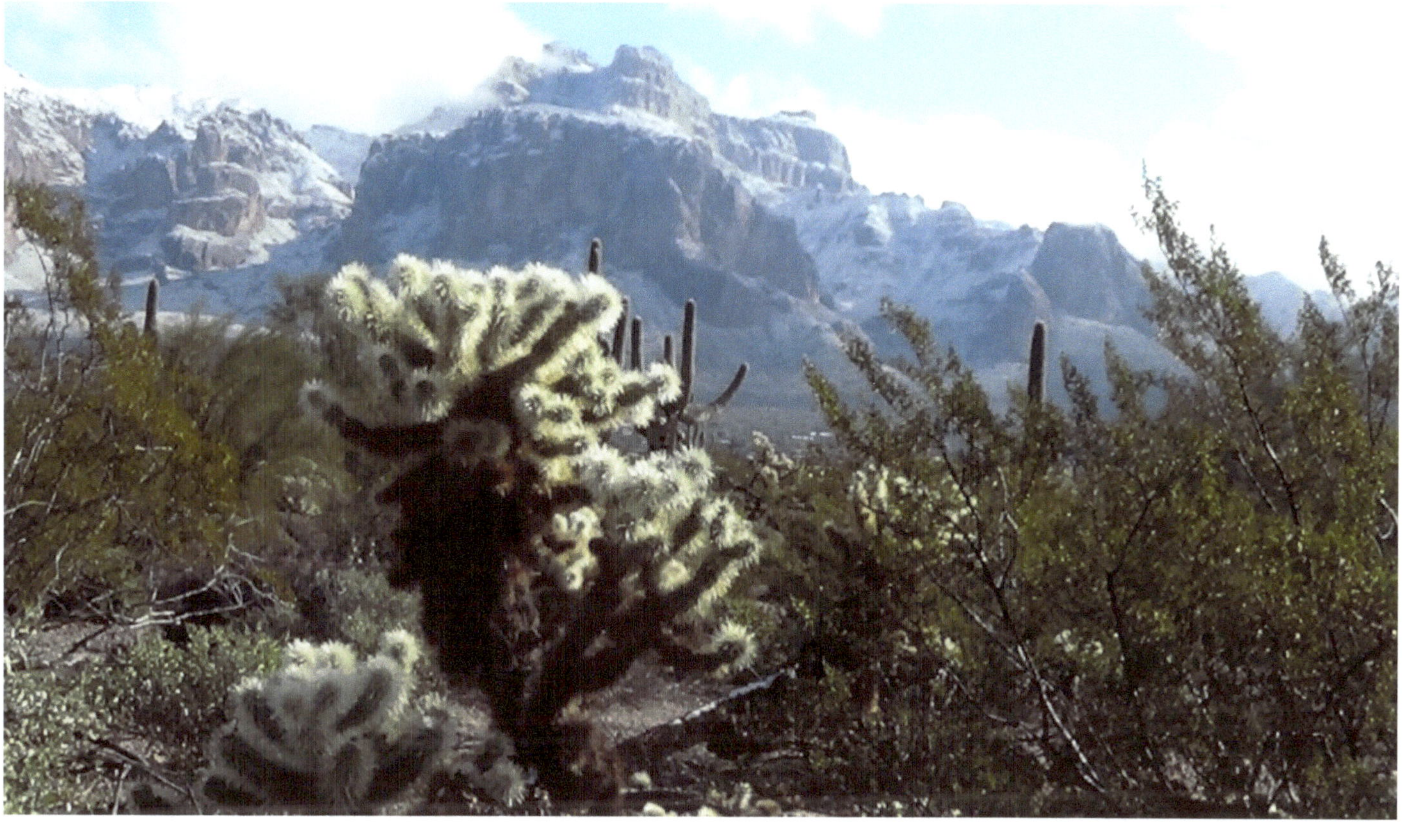

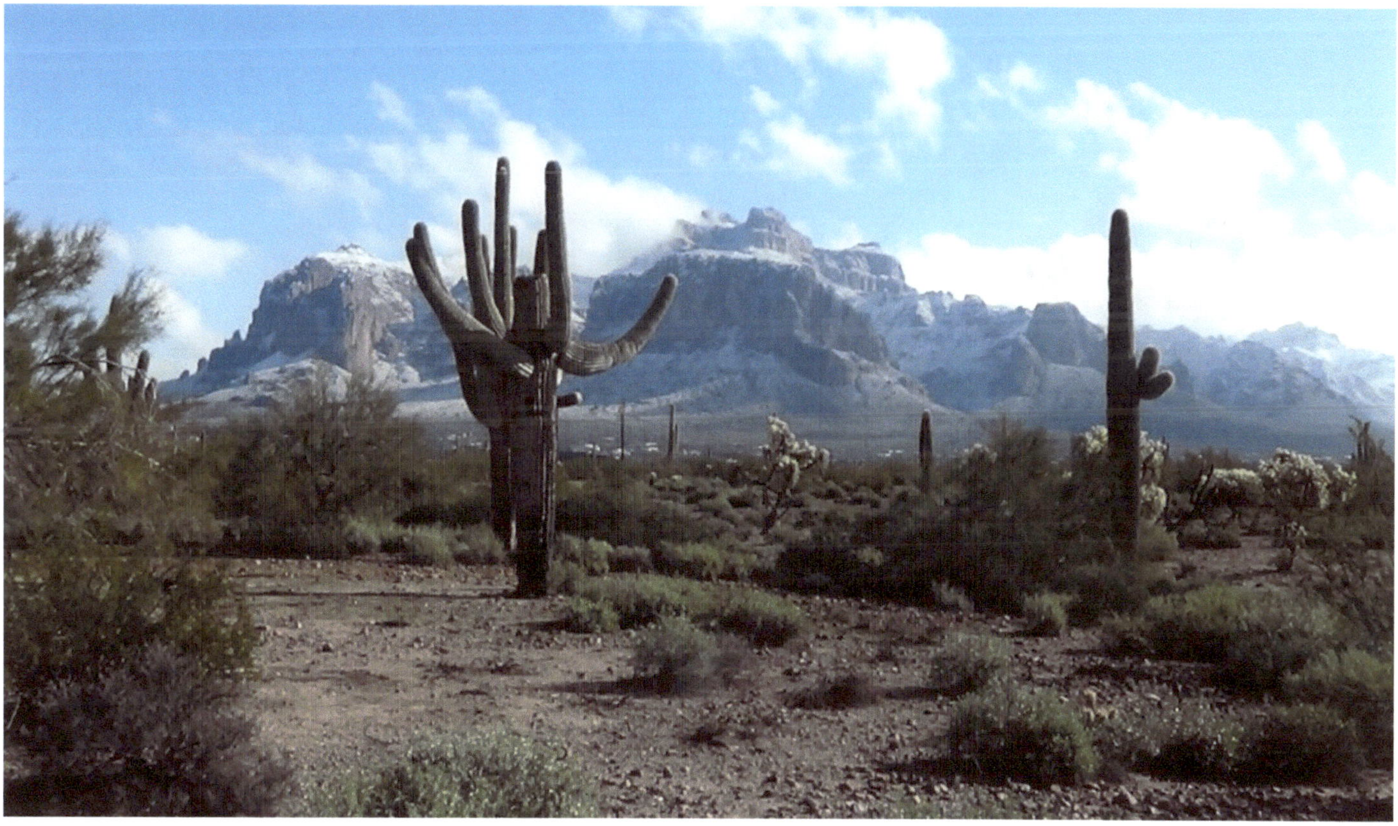

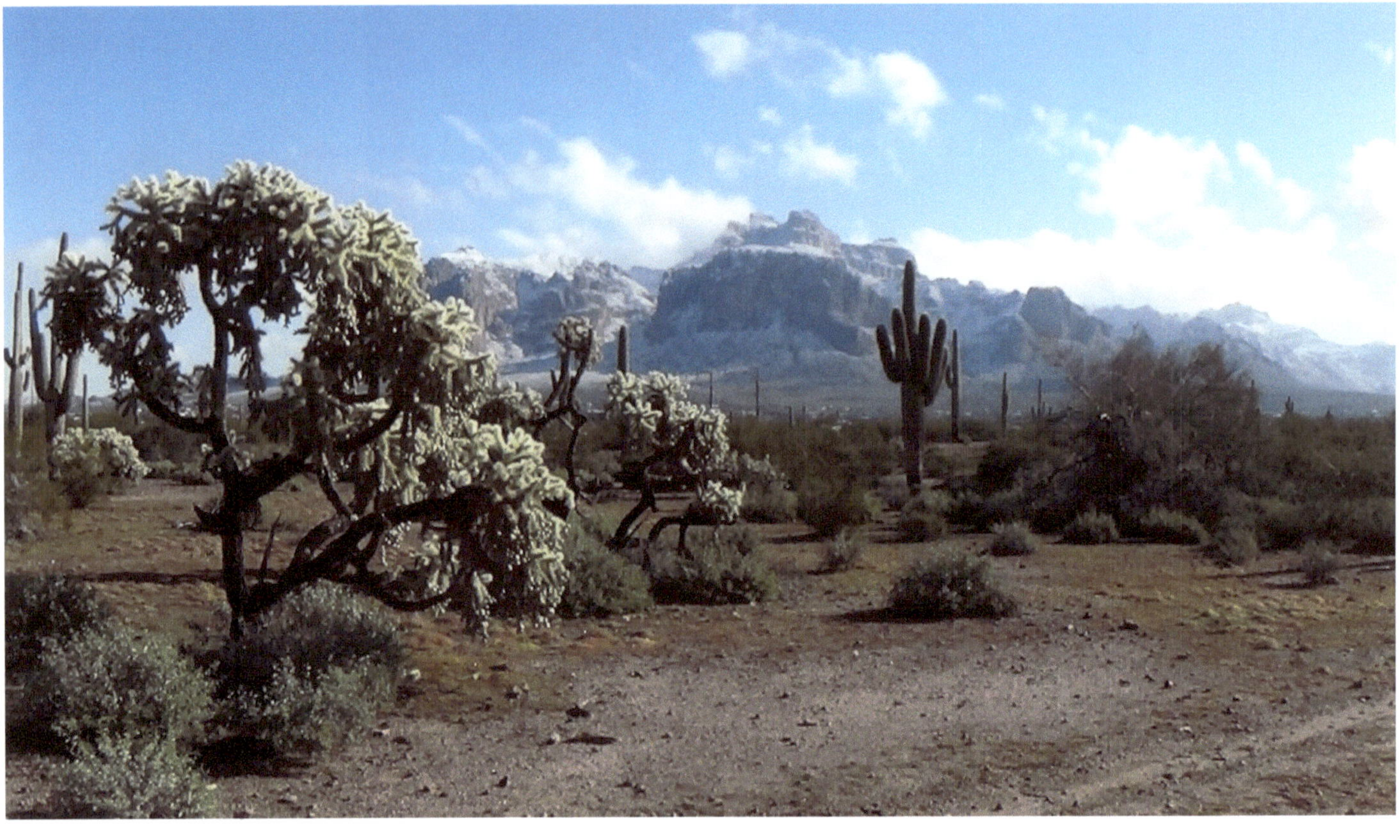

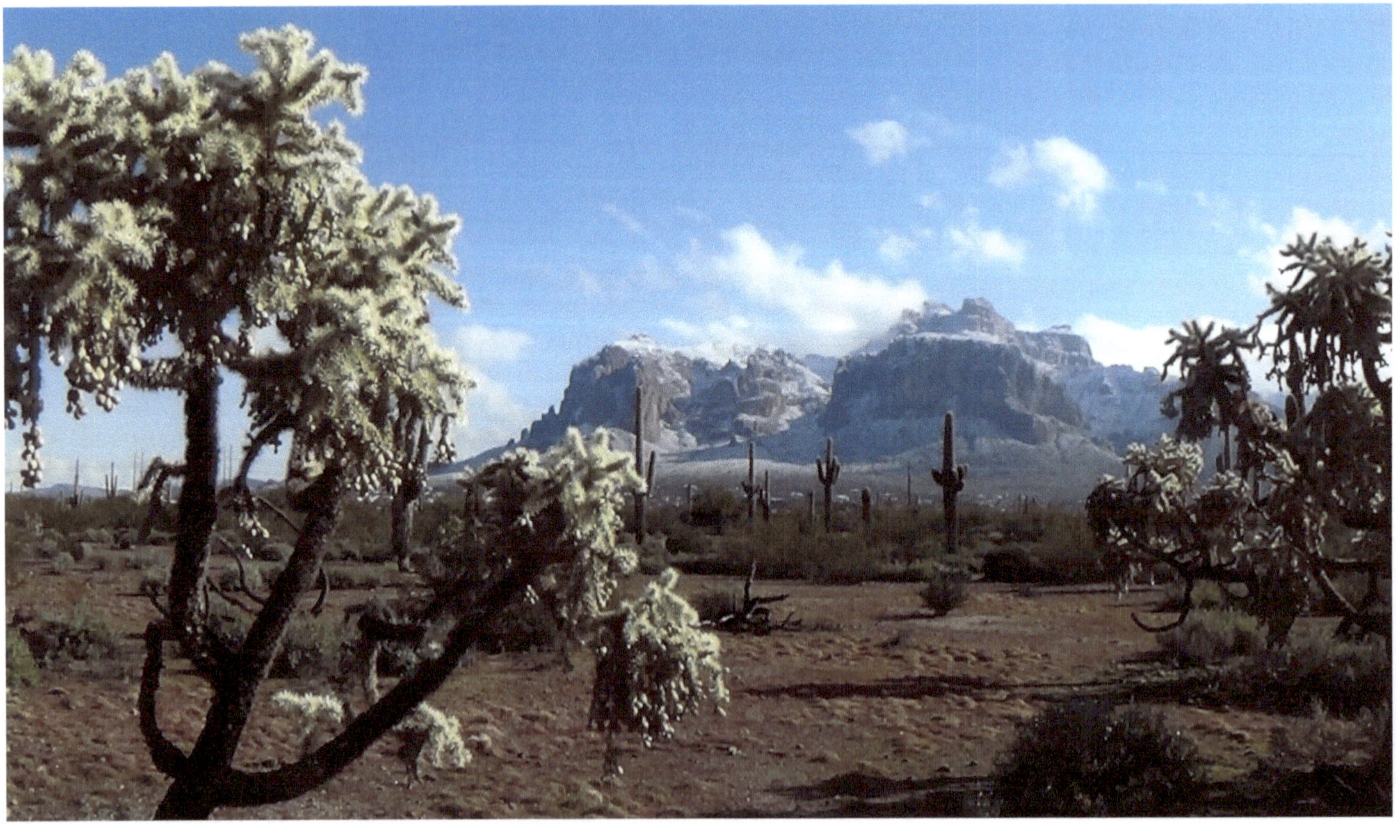

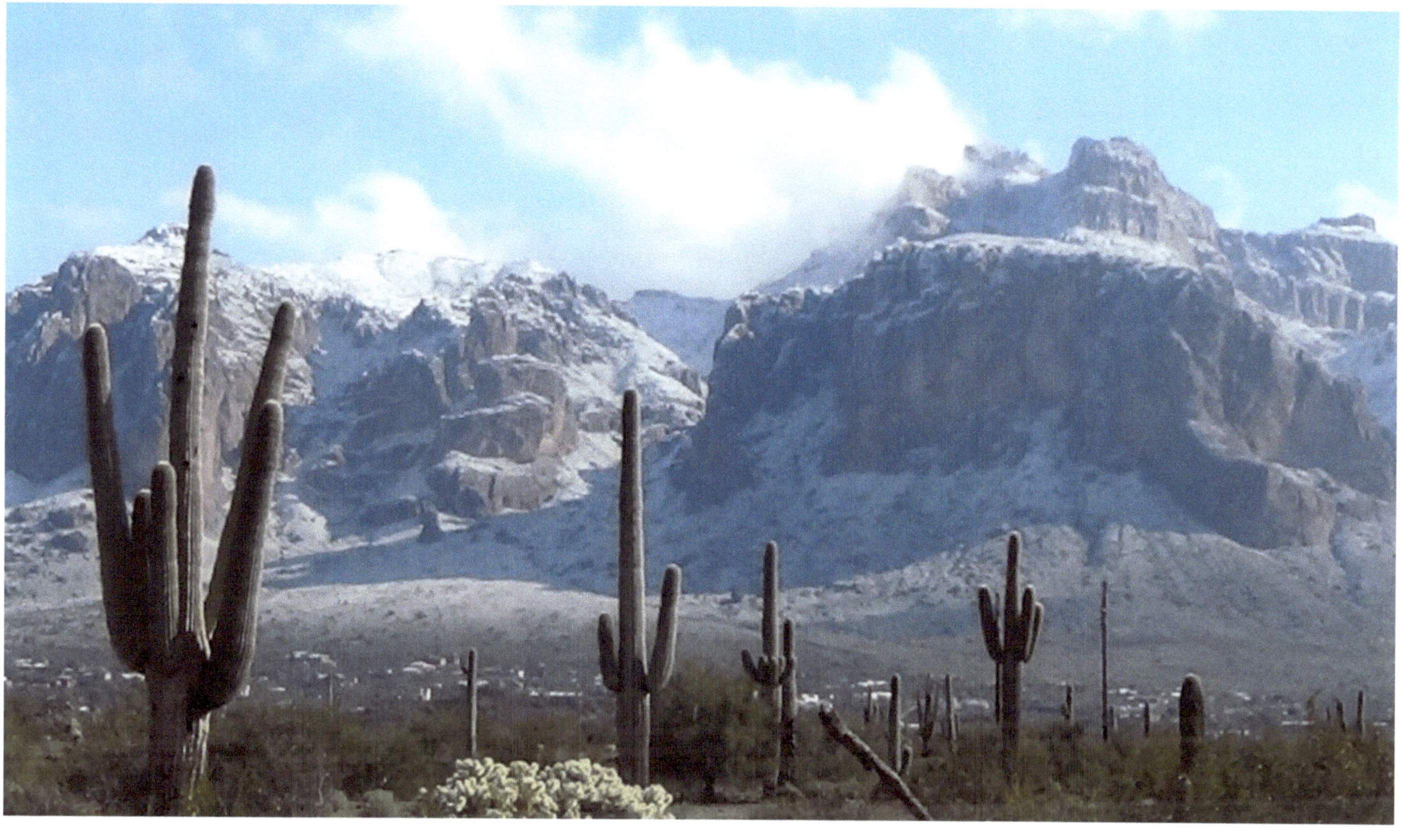

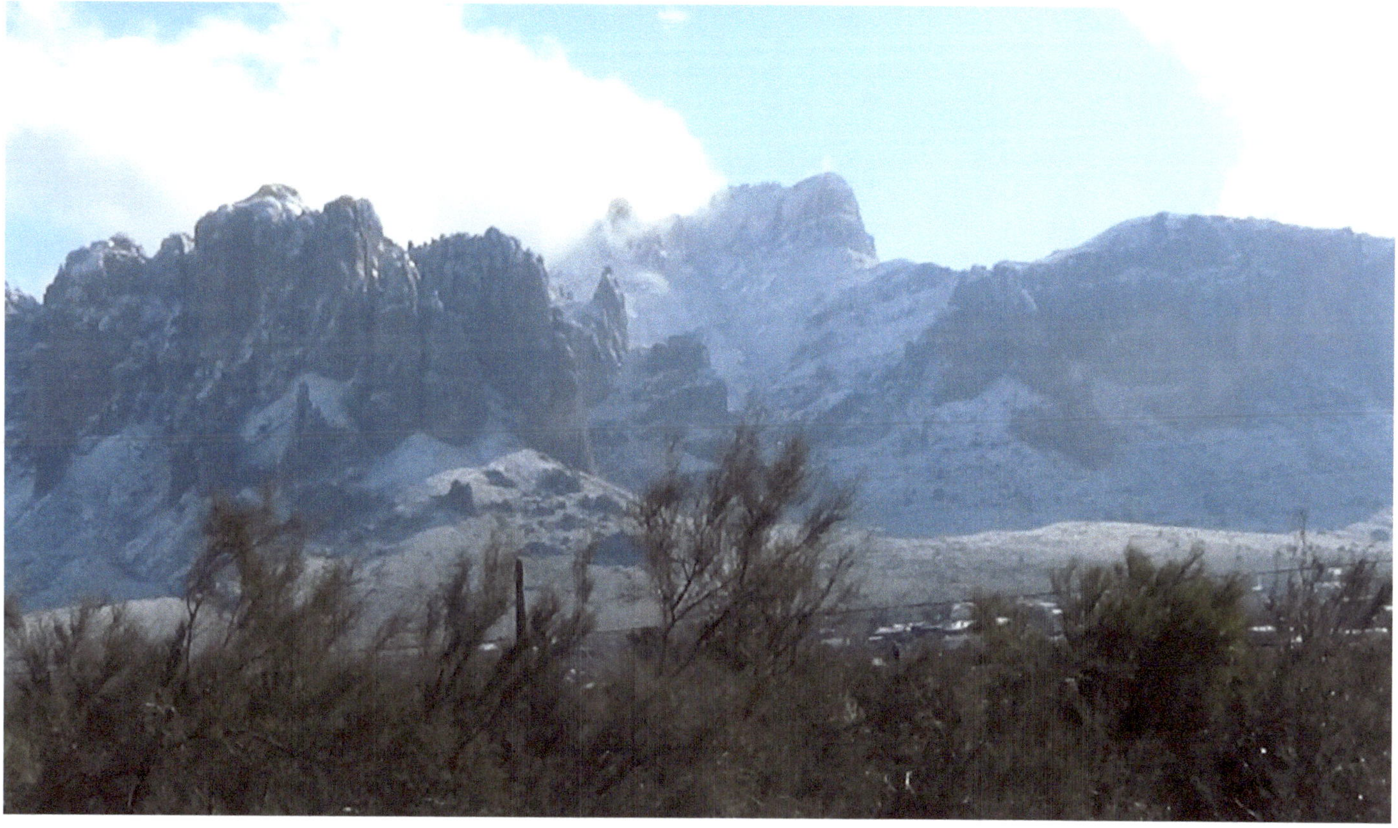

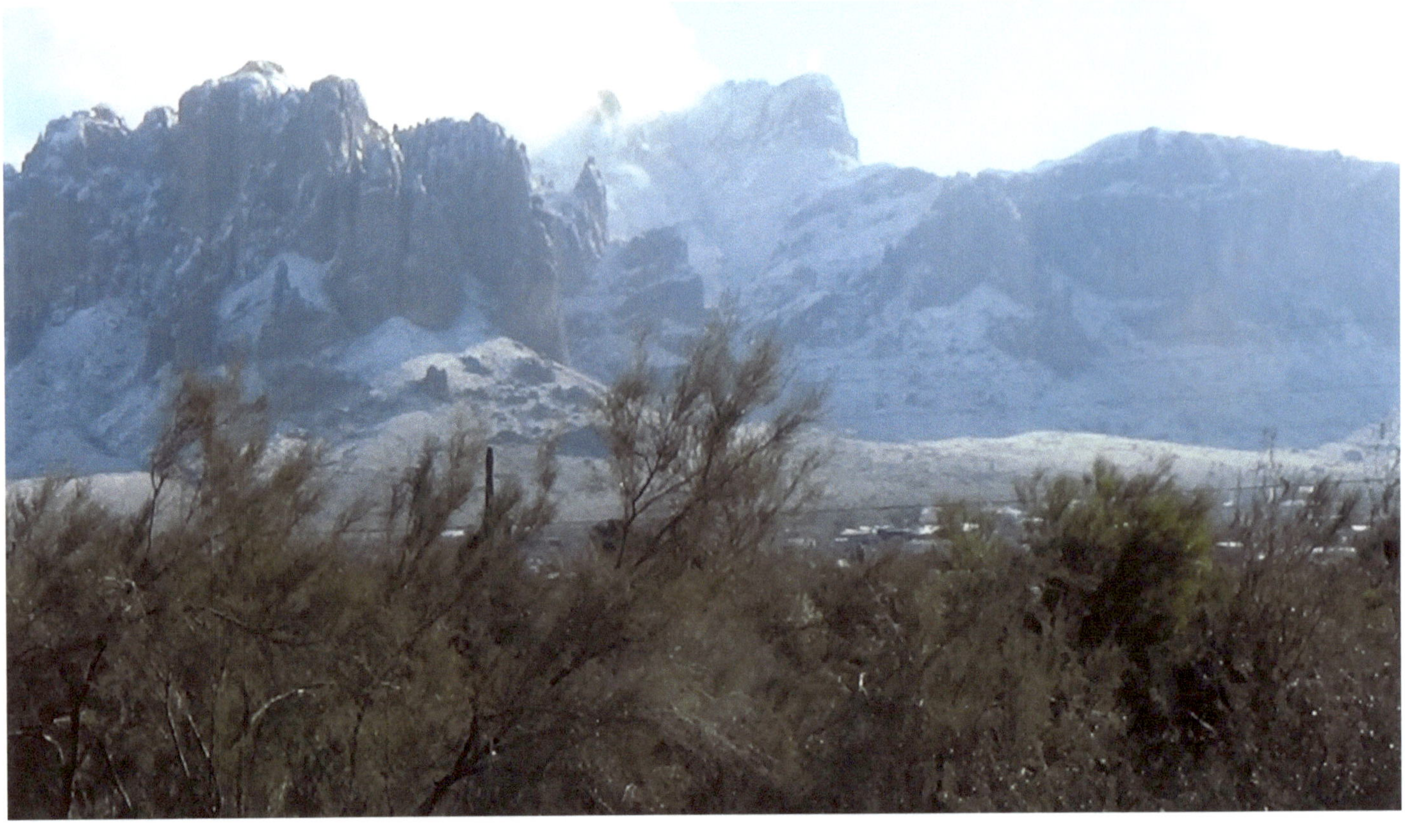

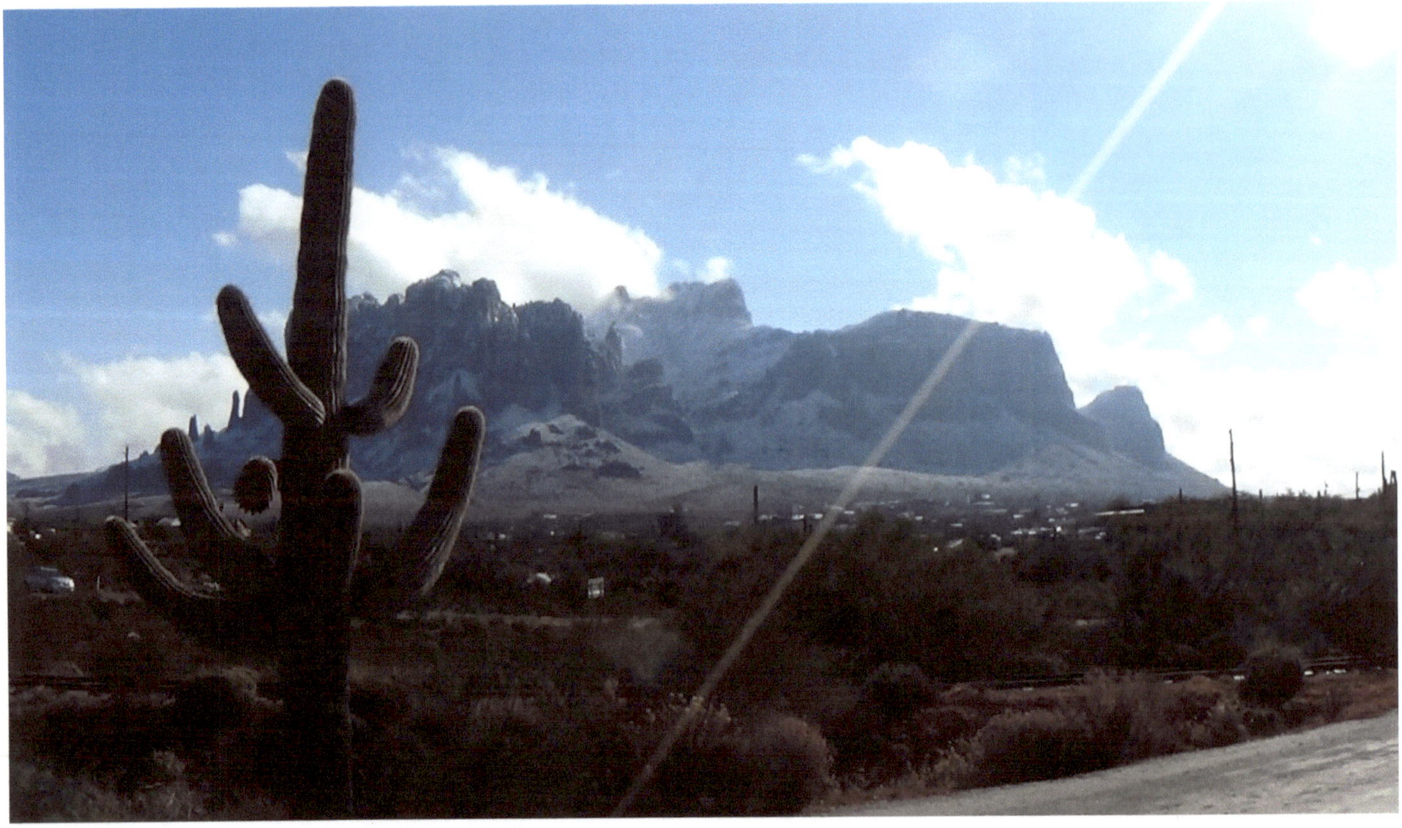

Just a few days later, it was gone. I am sure
Some warm winter's day in the desert I will
hear those beautiful words, "There is snow
on the mountain."

And the mountain is just as beautiful
without snow on it !

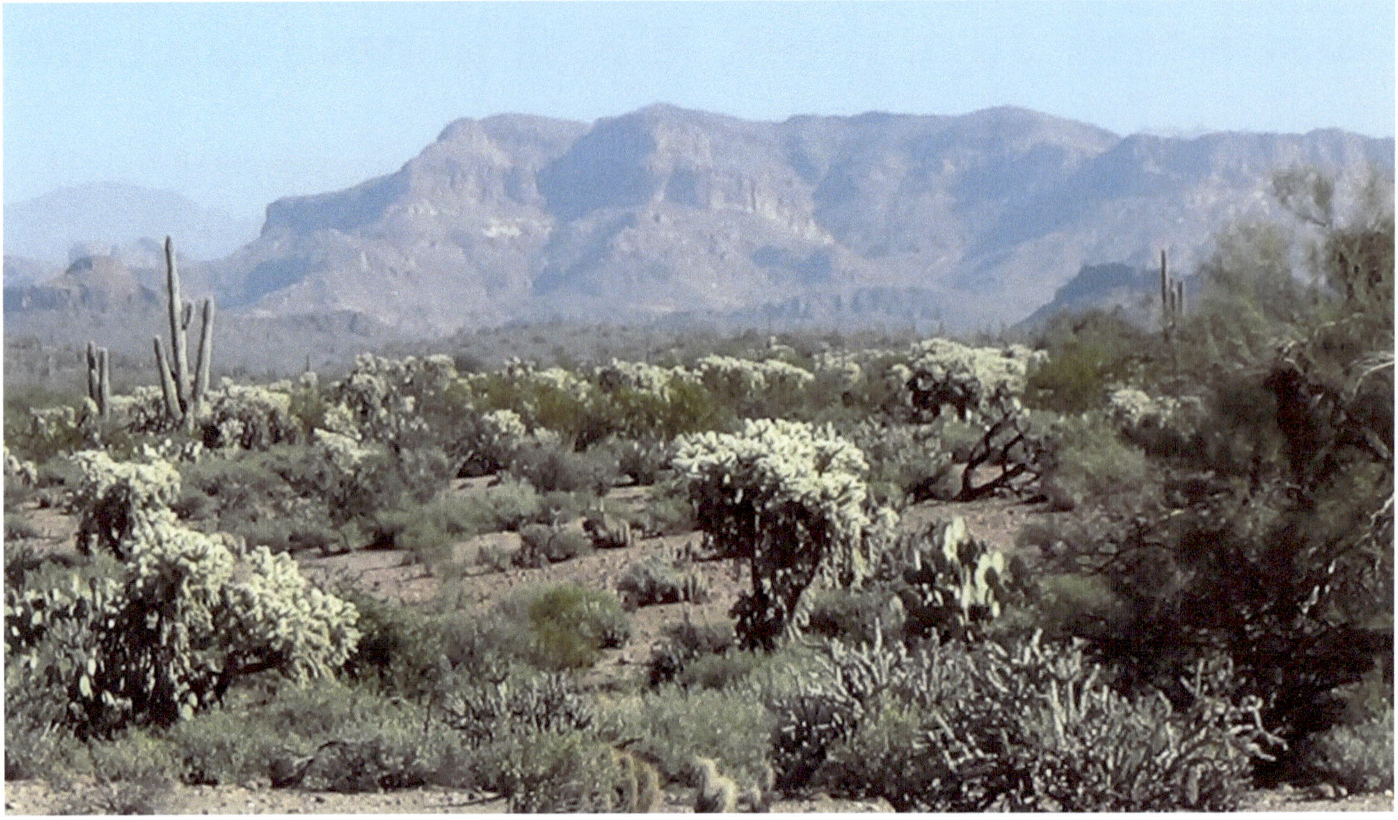

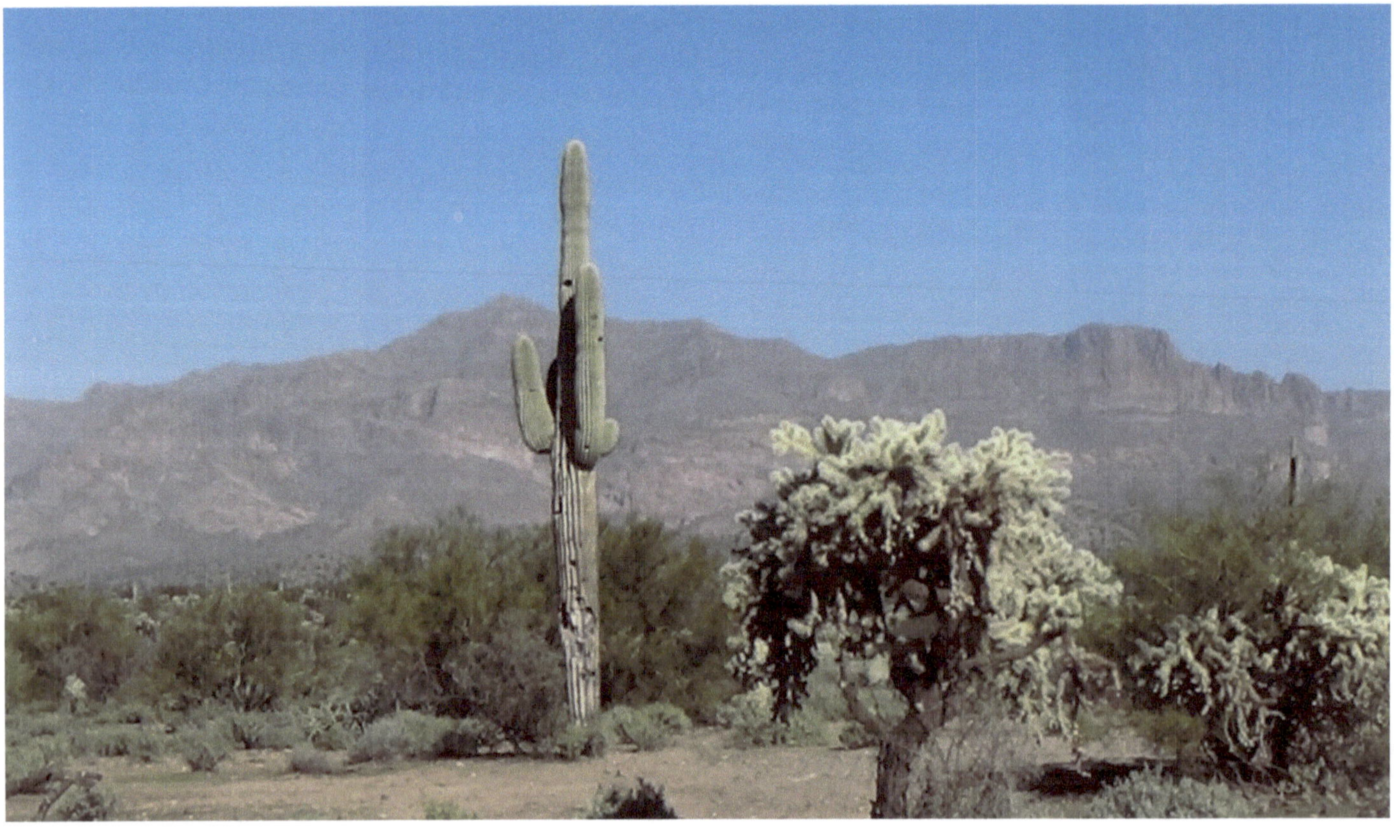

BE SURE TO CHECK OUT OTHER GREAT BOOK FORM NAM-VET PUBLISHING BY LARRY STIMELING'.

ALL Available at https://www.amazon.com/s/ref=nb_sb_noss_1?url=search-alias%3Daps&field-keywords=larry+stimeling

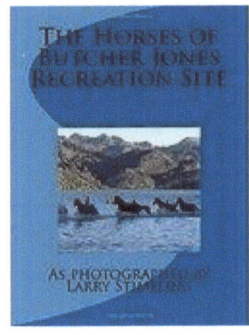

The Horses of Butcher Jones Recreation Site

Nov 13, 2015 | Large Print

by Larry Stimeling

Paperback

FREE Shipping on eligible orders

All proceeds form the sale of this book go to the SALT RIVER WILD HORSE MANAGAMENT GROUP a 501©3 Corporation.

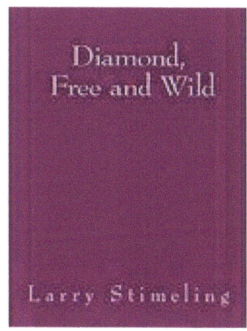

Diamond, Free and Wild

Jul 18, 2016

by Larry Stimeling

Paperback

FREE Shipping on eligible orders

All proceed from the sale of this book go to the SALT RIVER WILD HORSE
MANAGEMENT GROUP, A 501©3 Corporation.

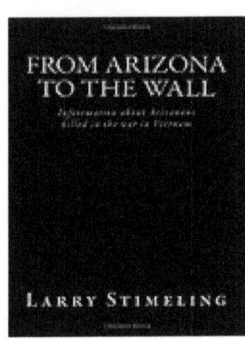

From Arizona to the Wall

Dec 7, 2015

by Larry Stimeling

Paperback

FREE Shipping on eligible orders

From The Wall Second Edition: Stories about people on the Wall

Nov 10, 2014

by Larry Stimeling

Paperback

FREE Shipping on eligible orders

DON'T TELL ME WE LOST
The sentiments of a Vietnam War veteran

LARRY STIMELING

Don't Tell Me We Lost: The sentiments of a Vietnam War veteran

Dec 24, 2015 | Large Print

by Larry Stimeling

Paperback